W9-APJ-375

vegetarian **dishes**

Easy dishes to cook at home

This edition published in 2010
LOVE FOOD is an imprint of Parragon Books Ltd

Parragon
Queen Street House
4 Queen Street
Bath BA1 1HE, UK

ISBN: 978-1-4075-8107-1

Printed in China

Designed by Talking Design
Introduction by Frances Eames

Notes for the Reader
This book uses imperial, metric, and US cup measurements. Follow the same units of measurement throughout; do not mix imperial and metric. All spoon measurements are level: teaspoons are assumed to be 5 ml, and tablespoons are assumed to be 15 ml. Unless otherwise stated, milk is assumed to be whole, eggs and individual vegetables such as potatoes are medium, and pepper is freshly ground black pepper.

The times given are an approximate guide only. Preparation times differ according to the techniques used by different people and the cooking times may also vary from those given as a result of the type of oven used. Optional ingredients, variations or serving suggestions have not been included in the calculations.

Recipes using raw or very lightly cooked eggs should be avoided by infants, the elderly, pregnant women, convalescents, and anyone with a chronic condition. Pregnant and breastfeeding women are advised to avoid eating peanuts and peanut products. Sufferers from nut allergies should be aware that some of the ready-prepared ingredients used in the recipes in this book may contain nuts. Always check the packaging before use. Vegetarians should be aware that some of the ready-prepared ingredients used in the recipes in this book may contain animal products. Always check the packaging before use.

Contents

introduction

The vegetarian lifestyle is one that more and more people are adopting, whether on a full-time or part-time basis. Gone are the days when vegetarianism was regarded as something of a fad—it is now recognized as a healthy, nutritious, and diverse approach to eating.

The most basic definition of a vegetarian is someone who doesn't eat meat, poultry, game, fish, shellfish or other seafood, or the by-products of slaughter, such as gelatin or animal fats. Most vegetarians choose to get their nutrients from a diet of fruit and vegetables, grains, nuts, beans, and seeds. Some vegetarians also include dairy products and eggs.

While some vegetarians make this choice for ethical and moral reasons and others for religious reasons, many vegetarians simply enjoy the culinary pleasure of eating plenty of flavorsome fresh vegetables and fruits. Whatever the reason, the popularity of vegetarianism is constantly increasing. Without a doubt a contributing factor to this increase in popularity is the range of fruit and vegetables that are readily available in today's modern shopping world. The selection is a far cry from the limited and often dull choices of years gone by. Everything from artichokes and squashes to eggplants and sweet potatoes can be easily sourced, meaning that the variety and combination of vegetarian meals is virtually endless.

Becoming A Vegetarian

If you are new to eating a meat-free diet, it can be comforting to know that many familiar, everyday dishes are, in fact, vegetarian—for example scrambled eggs, or cheese toasties. But if becoming a vegetarian seems to involve giving up all your favorite foods, make the change gradually. Rather than trying to change a lifetime of eating habits overnight, start by simply cutting out red meat for a couple of weeks, then progress to eliminating fish and shellfish and, finally, poultry. Then you can carry on slowly eliminating dairy products or other foods as you want. In a few short weeks you will quickly appreciate how old-fashioned the idea is that vegetarians only eat brown rice and salad greens!

Health Benefits Of A Vegetarian Lifestyle

One of the great appeals of a vegetarian diet is that you don't eat as many of the saturated fats found in animal products, fats that have been linked with some of the most deadly diseases of the modern age such as heart disease and various forms of cancer. As a vegetarian you will almost certainly eat more than the recommended 5–7 portions a day of fruit and vegetables which will ensure you receive those essential vitamins and antioxidants. A varied vegetarian diet will also be higher in fiber which is believed to help prevent constipation, bowel disorders, and other serious health problems.

Maintaining A Healthy Balance

Vegetarians, just like meat-eaters, need a variety of nutrients on a daily basis in order to function in tip-top form and remain healthy. And it is only by eating a wide variety of foods every day that you get all the nutrients you need naturally. A vegetarian diet should include a wide range of foods such as beans, cereals and grains, nuts and seeds, fruit, vegetables, dairy foods, soy products, and eggs. Following a balanced, healthy vegetarian eating plan, and including some foods from each group every day, should provide vegetarians with the correct balance of foods and all the nutrients, vitamins, and minerals that you need to keep healthy.

simple soups & **stunning salads**

Broccoli & Cheese
Soup

SERVES 6

2 tbsp butter
1 onion, chopped
1 lb/450 g potatoes, peeled and grated
2 fresh tarragon leaves
3 pints/1.7 liters vegetable stock
1 lb 8 oz /675 g broccoli, cut into small florets
6 oz/175 g cheddar cheese, grated
1 tbsp chopped fresh parsley
salt and pepper

Melt the butter in a large, heavy saucepan. Add the onion and cook, stirring occasionally, for 5 minutes, until soft. Add the grated potatoes and tarragon, season to taste with salt and pepper, and mix well. Pour in just enough of the stock to cover and bring to a boil. Lower the heat, cover, and simmer for 10 minutes.

Meanwhile, bring the remaining stock to a boil in another saucepan. Add the broccoli and cook for 6–8 minutes, until just tender.

Remove both pans from the heat, cool slightly, then ladle the contents of both pans into a blender or food processor. Process until smooth, then pour the mixture into a clean saucepan. Stir in the cheese, add the parsley, and heat gently to warm through, but do not let the soup boil. Ladle into warmed soup bowls and serve immediately.

Chickpea
Soup

SERVES 6

- generous 2¼ cups dried chickpeas, soaked in cold water overnight
- 2 tbsp olive oil
- 1 onion, finely chopped
- 2 garlic cloves, finely chopped
- 1 lb/450 g Swiss chard, trimmed and finely sliced
- 2 fresh rosemary sprigs
- 14 oz/400 g canned chopped tomatoes
- salt and pepper
- slices of toasted bread, to serve

Drain the chickpeas and put in a large saucepan. Cover with fresh cold water and bring to a boil, using a slotted spoon to skim off any foam that rises to the surface. Reduce the heat and simmer, uncovered, for 1–1¼ hours, or until tender, adding more water if necessary.

Drain the chickpeas, reserving the cooking water. Season the chickpeas well with salt and pepper. Put two-thirds in a food processor or blender with some of the reserved cooking water and process until smooth, adding more of the cooking water if necessary to give a thinner consistency. Return to the saucepan.

Heat the oil in a medium saucepan, then add the onion and garlic and cook over medium heat, stirring frequently, for 3–4 minutes, or until the onion has softened. Add the Swiss chard and rosemary sprigs and cook, stirring frequently, for 3–4 minutes. Add the tomatoes and remaining chickpeas and cook for an additional 5 minutes, or until the tomatoes have broken down to an almost smooth sauce. Remove the rosemary sprigs.

Add the Swiss chard and tomato mixture to the chickpea puree and simmer for 2–3 minutes. Taste and adjust the seasoning if necessary.

Serve in warmed soup bowls with warm slices of toasted bread on the side.

Celery Root Soup with Cheese Pastry Sticks

SERVES 4

- 3 tbsp olive oil
- 1 onion, chopped
- 1 celery root, peeled and cut into chunks
- 4 cups good-quality vegetable stock
- 1 small bunch fresh thyme, chopped; reserving whole sprigs, to garnish
- salt and pepper

Cheese Pastry Sticks

- butter, for greasing
- 13 oz/375 g puff pastry, thawed if frozen
- all-purpose flour, for dusting
- 1 egg, beaten
- 1 cup finely grated Parmesan cheese

Heat the oil in a large saucepan over medium heat, then add the onion and cook, stirring frequently, for 4–5 minutes, or until softened but not colored. Add the celery root and cook, stirring frequently, for 3–4 minutes. Pour in the stock and add the thyme. Simmer for 25 minutes, or until the celery root is tender.

Meanwhile, preheat the oven to 400°F/200°C. Lightly grease two baking sheets. For the pastry sticks, roll the pastry out thinly on a floured work surface. Brush with half the egg and scatter over half the Parmesan cheese. Add a good grinding of pepper. Fold the pastry in half. Brush with the remaining egg, then scatter with the remaining cheese and add another grinding of pepper. Cut into strips about ½ inch/1 cm wide. Twist the pastry strips gently along their length to produce spiral shapes. Bake in the preheated oven for 5 minutes, or until crisp and golden.

Transfer the soup to a food processor and process until smooth. Alternatively, use a handheld blender to process the soup until smooth in the saucepan. Gently reheat the soup in the saucepan. Season to taste with salt and pepper.

Pour the soup into warmed soup bowls, and garnish with thyme sprigs. Serve alongside the warm pastry sticks.

French Onion
Soup

SERVES 6

- 1 lb 8 oz/675 g onions
- 3 tbsp olive oil
- 4 garlic cloves, 3 chopped and 1 peeled and halved
- 1 tsp sugar
- 2 tsp chopped fresh thyme, plus extra sprigs to garnish
- 2 tbsp all-purpose flour
- ½ cup dry white wine
- 8½ cups vegetable stock
- 6 slices French bread
- 10½ oz/300 g Gruyère cheese, grated

Thinly slice the onions. Heat the oil in a large, heavy-bottom pan over medium–low heat, add the onions, and cook, stirring occasionally, for 10 minutes, or until they are just beginning to brown. Stir in the chopped garlic, sugar, and chopped thyme, then reduce the heat and cook, stirring occasionally, for 30 minutes, or until the onions are golden brown.

Sprinkle in the flour and cook, stirring constantly, for 1–2 minutes. Stir in the wine. Gradually stir in the stock and bring to a boil, skimming off any foam that rises to the surface, then reduce the heat and simmer for 45 minutes.

Meanwhile, preheat the broiler to medium. Toast the bread on both sides under the broiler, then rub the toast with the cut edges of the halved garlic clove.

Ladle the soup into 6 ovenproof bowls set on a baking sheet. Float a piece of toast in each bowl and divide the grated cheese among them. Place under the broiler for 2–3 minutes, or until the cheese has just melted. Garnish with thyme sprigs and serve immediately.

Mozzarella Salad with *Sun-dried Tomatoes*

SERVES 4

3½ oz/100 g mixed salad greens, such as oak leaf lettuce, baby spinach, and arugula
1 lb 2 oz/500 g smoked mozzarella cheese, sliced

Dressing

5 oz/140 g sun-dried tomatoes in olive oil (drained weight), reserving the oil from the jar
¼ cup coarsely shredded fresh basil
¼ cup coarsely chopped fresh flat-leaf parsley
1 tbsp capers, rinsed
1 tbsp balsamic vinegar
1 garlic clove, coarsely chopped
olive oil, if necessary
pepper

For the dressing, put the sun-dried tomatoes, basil, parsley, capers, vinegar, and garlic in a food processor or blender. Measure the oil from the sun-dried tomatoes jar and make it up to ⅔ cup with more olive oil if necessary. Add it to the food processor or blender and process until smooth. Season to taste with pepper.

Divide the salad greens among 4 individual serving plates. Top with the slices of mozzarella and spoon the dressing over them. Serve immediately.

Feta, Mint & Strawberry

Salad with Green Beans & Pistachios

SERVES 4–6

1 lb 2 oz/500 g fine green beans
1 lb 2 oz/500 g strawberries
2–3 tbsp pistachios
1 small bunch fresh mint leaves
1 lb 2 oz/500 g feta cheese (drained weight)
salt and pepper

Dressing

2 tbsp raspberry vinegar
2 tsp superfine sugar
1 tbsp Dijon mustard
pinch of salt
½ cup olive oil

For the dressing, mix the vinegar, sugar, mustard, and salt together in a bowl until smooth. Slowly pour in the oil, whisking constantly until the mixture has emulsified. Cover and refrigerate until required.

Blanch the beans in a large saucepan of salted boiling water for 1–2 minutes, so that they retain plenty of crunch. Drain and quickly toss in a large, cool bowl. Hull and halve the strawberries, then add to the beans. Stir in the pistachios and mint leaves. Toss the salad with enough of the dressing to coat lightly.

Break the feta cheese into chunks and scatter over the salad. Add a good grinding of pepper and serve immediately.

Warm Pasta *Salad*

SERVES 4

8 oz/225 g dried farfalle or other pasta shapes
6 pieces of sun-dried tomato in oil, drained and chopped
4 scallions, chopped
1¼ cups arugula, shredded
½ cucumber, seeded and diced
salt and pepper

Dressing

4 tbsp olive oil
1 tbsp white wine vinegar
½ tsp superfine sugar
1 tsp Dijon mustard
salt and pepper
4 fresh basil leaves, finely shredded

For the dressing, whisk the olive oil, vinegar, sugar, and mustard together in a bowl or pitcher. Season to taste with salt and pepper and stir in the basil.

Bring a large heavy-bottom pan of lightly salted water to a boil. Add the pasta, return to a boil, and cook for 8–10 minutes, or until tender but still firm to the bite. Drain and transfer to a salad bowl. Add the dressing and toss well.

Add the tomatoes, scallions, arugula, and cucumber, season to taste with salt and pepper, and toss. Serve warm.

appetizers

Hot Garlic-Stuffed Mushrooms

SERVES 4

4 large portobello mushrooms
olive oil, for brushing
2–3 garlic cloves, crushed
2 shallots
½ cup fresh whole wheat breadcrumbs
few fresh basil sprigs, plus extra to garnish
scant ¼ cup plumped dried apricots, chopped
1 tbsp pine nuts
2 oz/55 g feta cheese
pepper

Preheat the oven to 350°F/180°C. Remove the stalks from the mushrooms and set aside. Brush the mushrooms with the olive oil and place in a roasting pan. Cook for 1 minute and then turn the mushrooms over and cook for an additional minute.

Put the mushroom stalks in a food processor with the garlic, shallots, and breadcrumbs. Set aside a few basil sprigs for the garnish then place the remainder in the food processor with the apricots, pine nuts, and feta cheese. Add pepper to taste.

Process for 1–2 minutes, or until a stuffing consistency is formed, then divide among the mushroom caps.

Bake for 10–12 minutes, or until the mushrooms are tender and the stuffing is crisp on the top. Serve garnished with the reserved basil sprigs.

Tomato & Potato
Tortilla

SERVES 6

- 2 lb 4 oz/1 kg potatoes, peeled and cut into small cubes
- 2 tbsp olive oil
- 1 bunch of scallions, chopped
- 4 oz/115 g cherry tomatoes, halved
- 6 eggs
- 3 tbsp water
- 2 tbsp chopped fresh parsley
- salt and pepper

Cook the potatoes in a saucepan of lightly salted boiling water for 8–10 minutes, or until tender. Drain and set aside until required.

Preheat the broiler to medium. Heat the oil in a large skillet with a heatproof handle. Add the scallions and cook until just softened. Add the potatoes and cook for 3–4 minutes, until coated with oil and hot. Smooth the top and sprinkle the tomatoes throughout.

Mix the eggs, water, parsley, and seasoning in a bowl, then pour into the skillet. Cook over very gentle heat for 10–15 minutes, until the tortilla looks fairly set.

Place the skillet under the hot broiler and cook until the top is brown and set. Cool for 10–15 minutes before sliding out of the skillet onto a cutting board. Cut into wedges and serve at once.

Red Bell Pepper & Zucchini *Stacks*

SERVES 6

- 2 tsp olive oil
- 1 small red bell pepper, seeded and finely chopped
- generous 3/4 cup finely chopped zucchini
- 1 garlic clove, crushed
- scant 1/4 cup finely chopped sun-dried tomatoes in oil, patted dry
- 1–2 tbsp finely shredded fresh basil leaves, plus extra to garnish
- 4 tbsp prepared smooth tomato salsa or classic green pesto
- 18 chilled fresh small/mini (cocktail) blinis (2 1/4–2 1/2 inches/ 5.5–6 cm in diameter)
- 1/2 cup grated mozzarella or cheddar cheese
- 1/4 cup finely grated Parmesan cheese
- 5 tbsp thick sour cream or crème fraîche
- salt and pepper

Preheat the oven to 350°F/180°C. Lightly grease a cookie sheet and set aside. Heat the olive oil in a small pan over medium–high heat. Add the bell pepper, zucchini, and garlic and sauté for 4–5 minutes.

Remove from the heat and stir in the sun-dried tomatoes, shredded basil, and seasoning, mixing well. Set aside. Spread 1/2 teaspoon of salsa on one side of each blini. To assemble the stacks, place one blini, coated-side up, on a cutting board. Spoon a little (about 1 heaping tablespoon) of the sautéed vegetable mixture on top of the blini and level the surface. Sprinkle a little mozzarella cheese over the vegetables. Place a second blini on top, coated-side up, top with a spoonful of the vegetable mixture, and level the surface, then sprinkle with mozzarella. Place a third blini on top, coated-side up. Place the blini stack on the prepared cookie sheet.

Repeat this procedure with the remaining blinis, sautéed vegetables, and mozzarella to make a total of 6 blinis stacks. Sprinkle the Parmesan cheese evenly over the top of the blinis stacks. Bake for 8–10 minutes, until the blinis are hot and the cheese is melting. Meanwhile, combine the sour cream and the remaining salsa in a small bowl. Garnish the cooked blinis stacks with a sprinkling of shredded basil and serve immediately with a spoonful of salsa-flavored sour cream on top or on the side.

Glazed Vegetable *Kebabs*

SERVES 4

- 2/3 cup lowfat plain yogurt
- 4 tbsp mango chutney
- 1 tsp chopped garlic
- 1 tbsp lemon juice
- 8 baby onions, peeled
- 16 baby corn, halved
- 2 zucchini, cut into 1-inch/ 2.5-cm pieces
- 16 white mushrooms
- 16 cherry tomatoes
- salt and pepper
- salad greens, to garnish

If using wooden skewers, presoak them for 30 minutes to prevent burning under the broiler. Put the yogurt, chutney, garlic, lemon juice, salt, and pepper in a bowl and stir together.

Put the onions in a pan of boiling water. Return to a boil, then drain well.

Thread the onions, corn, zucchini, mushrooms, and tomatoes alternately onto 8 metal or wooden skewers.

Arrange the kebabs on a broiler pan and brush with the yogurt glaze. Cook under a preheated broiler for 10 minutes, turning and brushing frequently, until golden and tender.

Serve with a garnish of mixed salad greens.

Vegetable
Tartlets

MAKES 12

butter, for greasing
12 ready-baked pastry shells
2 tbsp olive oil
1 red bell pepper, seeded and diced
1 garlic clove, crushed
1 small onion, finely chopped
8 oz/225 g ripe tomatoes, chopped
1 tbsp torn fresh basil
1 tsp fresh or dried thyme
salt and pepper
green salad, to serve

Preheat the oven to 400°F/200°C and grease several baking sheets.

Place the ready-baked pastry shells on the prepared baking sheets.

Heat the oil in a skillet, add the bell pepper, garlic, and onion, and cook over high heat for about 3 minutes until soft.

Add the tomatoes, herbs, and seasoning and spoon onto the pastry shells.

Bake for about 5 minutes, or until the filling is piping hot. Serve warm with a green salad.

Pumpkin *Soufflé*

SERVES 4–6

- 2⅔ cups diced pumpkin
- 2 tbsp butter, diced, plus extra for greasing
- 2 tbsp finely grated Parmesan cheese
- ¼ cup all-purpose flour
- generous 1 cup milk
- 4 eggs, separated, plus 1 extra egg white
- 1 cup finely grated sharp cheddar cheese
- 1 tsp Dijon mustard
- salt and pepper
- cooked fresh vegetables, to serve

Cook the pumpkin in a pan of boiling water for about 10 minutes, until tender. Drain well, then mash the flesh and set aside. Preheat the oven to 375°F/190°C. Grease a 2¾-quart/2½-liter, 8-inch/20-cm soufflé dish with butter, then sprinkle with the Parmesan, coating the bottom and sides evenly. Set aside. Put the diced butter, flour, and milk in a pan and heat gently, whisking constantly, until the sauce comes to a boil and thickens. Simmer for 3 minutes, stirring.

Transfer the sauce to a large bowl, add the mashed pumpkin, and mix well. Gradually beat in the egg yolks and all but 2 tablespoons of the cheddar cheese, then stir in the mustard, and season with salt and pepper. Place a cookie sheet in the oven to preheat. Whisk the egg whites in a separate, clean, dry bowl until stiff (this is easiest to do with an electric handheld mixer), then carefully fold them into the pumpkin mixture.

Pour the mixture gently into the prepared dish and sprinkle with the remaining cheddar. Stand the dish on the cookie sheet in the oven and bake for 25–30 minutes, until well risen, golden brown, and lightly set (just firm to the touch). Serve immediately with cooked fresh vegetables, such as green beans and broccoli florets.

mighty **mains**

Sweet Potato Ravioli with *Sage Butter*

SERVES 4

Pasta

14 oz/400 g type 00 pasta flour
4 eggs, beaten
semolina, for dusting
salt

Filling

1 lb 2 oz/500 g sweet potatoes
3 tbsp olive oil
1 large onion, finely chopped
1 garlic clove, crushed
1 tsp fresh thyme leaves, chopped
2 tbsp runny honey
salt and pepper

Sage Butter

scant ½ stick butter
1 bunch fresh sage leaves finely chopped, reserving a few leaves to garnish

For the pasta, sift the flour into a large bowl or food processor. Add the eggs and bring the mixture together to make a soft but not sticky dough. Turn out onto a work surface lightly dusted with semolina and knead for 4–5 minutes.

For the filling, peel the sweet potatoes and cut into chunks. Cook in a saucepan of boiling water for 20 minutes, or until tender. Drain and mash. Heat the oil in a skillet over medium heat, then add the onion and cook, stirring frequently, for 4–5 minutes. Stir the onion into the mashed potatoes and add the garlic and thyme leaves. Drizzle with the honey and season.

Using a pasta machine, roll the pasta out to a thickness of about ⅓ inch/7 mm (or use a rolling pin on a work surface lightly dusted with semolina). Cut the pasta in half. Place teaspoonfuls of the filling at evenly spaced intervals across one half of the pasta. Brush around the filling with a small amount of water and cover with the second half. Press lightly around the filling to seal the pasta and cut into squares with a sharp knife.

Bring a large saucepan of salted water to a boil and drop in the ravioli. Cook for 2–3 minutes until the pasta rises to the surface and is tender but still retaining a little bite. Meanwhile, for the sage butter, melt the butter with the sage in a small saucepan over gentle heat. Drain the ravioli and immediately toss with the sage butter. Garnish with sage leaves.

Cauliflower, Eggplant & Green Bean Korma

SERVES 4–6

scant ⅔ cup cashews
1½ tbsp garlic and ginger paste
generous ¾ cup water
4 tbsp ghee, vegetable oil, or peanut oil
1 large onion, chopped
5 green cardamom pods, lightly crushed
1 cinnamon stick, broken in half
¼ tsp ground turmeric
generous 1 cup heavy cream
5 oz/140 g new potatoes, scrubbed and chopped into ½-inch/1-cm pieces
5 oz/140 g cauliflower florets
½ tsp garam masala
5 oz/140 g eggplant, chopped into chunks
5 oz/140 g green beans, chopped into ½-inch/1-cm pieces
salt and pepper
fresh mint or cilantro, chopped, to garnish

Heat a large, flameproof casserole or skillet with a tight-fitting lid over high heat. Add the cashews and stir until they start to brown, then tip them out of the casserole into a spice blender. Add the garlic and ginger paste and 1 tablespoon of the water, and process until a coarse paste forms.

Melt the ghee in the casserole over medium–high heat. Add the onion and cook for 5–8 minutes, or until golden brown. Add the nut paste and stir for 5 minutes.

Stir in the cardamom pods, cinnamon stick, and turmeric. Add the cream and the remaining water and bring to a boil, stirring. Reduce the heat to the lowest level, cover the casserole, and simmer for 5 minutes.

Add the potatoes, cauliflower, and garam masala and simmer, covered, for 5 minutes. Stir in the eggplant and green beans and continue simmering for an additional 5 minutes, or until all the vegetables are tender. Check the sauce occasionally to make sure it isn't sticking on the bottom of the pan, and stir in extra water if needed.

Taste and add seasoning, if necessary. Sprinkle with the mint to serve.

Parsnip & Tomato
Casserole

SERVES 4

- 3 tbsp olive oil
- 1 lb 5 oz/600 g parsnips, peeled and thinly sliced
- 1 tsp fresh thyme leaves
- 1 tsp superfine sugar
- 1¼ cups heavy cream
- 1 lb 5 oz/600 g tomatoes, thinly sliced
- 1 tsp dried oregano
- 1½ cups grated cheddar cheese
- salt and pepper

Preheat the oven to 350°F/180°C.

Heat the oil in a skillet over medium heat, then add the parsnips, thyme, sugar, and salt and pepper to taste and cook, stirring frequently, for 6–8 minutes, or until golden and softened.

Spread half the parsnips over the bottom of a gratin dish. Pour over half the cream, then arrange half the tomatoes in an even layer across the parsnips. Season to taste with salt and pepper and scatter over half the oregano. Sprinkle over half the cheddar cheese. Top with the remaining parsnips and tomatoes. Sprinkle with the remaining oregano, then season to taste with salt and pepper and pour over the remaining cream. Scatter over the remaining cheese.

Cover with foil and bake in the preheated oven for 40 minutes, or until the parsnips are tender. Remove the foil and return to the oven for an additional 5–10 minutes, or until the top is golden and bubbling. Serve immediately.

Parmesan Cheese
Risotto with Mushrooms

SERVES 4

4 cups vegetable stock or chicken stock
2 tbsp olive oil or vegetable oil
generous 1 cup risotto rice
2 garlic cloves, crushed
1 onion, chopped
2 celery stalks, chopped
1 red or green bell pepper, seeded and chopped
8 oz/225 g mushrooms, thinly sliced
1 tbsp chopped fresh oregano or 1 tsp dried oregano
¼ cup sun-dried tomatoes in olive oil, drained and chopped (optional)
½ cup finely grated Parmesan cheese
salt and pepper
fresh flat-leaf parsley sprigs or fresh bay leaves, to garnish

Bring the stock to a boil in a saucepan, then reduce the heat and keep simmering gently over low heat while you are cooking the risotto.

Heat the oil in a deep skillet or saucepan. Add the rice and cook over low heat, stirring constantly, for 2–3 minutes, until the grains are thoroughly coated in oil and translucent.

Add the garlic, onion, celery, and bell pepper and cook, stirring frequently, for 5 minutes. Add the mushrooms and cook for 3–4 minutes. Stir in the oregano.

Gradually add the hot stock, a ladleful at a time. Stir constantly and add more liquid as the rice absorbs each addition. Increase the heat to medium so that the liquid bubbles. Cook for 20 minutes, or until all the liquid is absorbed and the rice is creamy. Add the sun-dried tomatoes, if using, 5 minutes before the end of the cooking time and season to taste with salt and pepper.

Remove the risotto from the heat and stir in half the Parmesan cheese until it melts. Transfer the risotto to warmed plates. Top with the remaining cheese, garnish with flat-leaf parsley, and serve at once.

Rigatoni with Bell Peppers & Goat Cheese

SERVES 4

- 2 tbsp olive oil
- 1 tbsp butter
- 1 small onion, finely chopped
- 4 bell peppers, yellow and red, seeded and cut into 3/4-inch/2-cm squares
- 3 garlic cloves, thinly sliced
- 1 lb/450 g dried rigatoni (pasta tubes)
- 4½ oz/125 g goat cheese, crumbled
- 15 fresh basil leaves, shredded
- 10 black olives, pitted and sliced
- salt and pepper

Heat the oil and butter in a large skillet over medium heat. Add the onion and cook until soft. Raise the heat to medium–high and add the bell peppers and garlic. Cook for 12–15 minutes, stirring, until the peppers are tender but not mushy. Season to taste with salt and pepper. Remove from the heat.

Bring a large saucepan of lightly salted water to a boil. Add the pasta, bring back to a boil, and cook for 8–10 minutes, or until tender but still firm to the bite. Drain and transfer to a warmed serving dish. Add the goat cheese and toss to mix.

Briefly reheat the sauce. Add the basil and olives. Pour over the pasta and toss well to mix. Serve immediately.

Tomato *Ratatouille*

SERVES 4

- 2 tbsp olive oil
- 1 onion, cut into small wedges
- 2–4 garlic cloves, chopped
- 1 small eggplant, trimmed and chopped
- 1 small red bell pepper, seeded and chopped
- 1 small yellow bell pepper, seeded and chopped
- 1 zucchini, trimmed and chopped
- 2 tbsp tomato paste
- 3 tbsp water
- 4 oz/115 g mushrooms, sliced if large
- 8 oz/225 g ripe tomatoes, chopped
- pepper
- 1 tbsp shredded fresh basil, to garnish
- 1 oz/25 g Parmesan cheese, freshly shaved, to serve

Heat the oil in a heavy-bottom pan, add the onion, garlic, and eggplant and cook, stirring frequently for 3 minutes.

Add the peppers and zucchini. Mix the tomato paste and water together in a small bowl and stir into the pan. Bring to a boil, cover with a lid, reduce the heat to a simmer, and cook for 10 minutes.

Add the mushrooms and chopped tomatoes with pepper to taste and continue to simmer for 12–15 minutes, stirring occasionally, until the vegetables are tender.

Divide the ratatouille among 4 warmed bowls, garnish each with shredded basil, and serve with freshly shaved Parmesan cheese to sprinkle over.

something **on the side**

Roasted Root *Vegetables*

SERVES 4–6

- 3 parsnips, cut into 2-inch/5-cm chunks
- 4 baby turnips, quartered
- 3 carrots, cut into 2-inch/5-cm chunks
- 1 lb/450 g butternut squash, peeled and cut into 2-inch/5-cm chunks
- 1 lb/450 g sweet potatoes, peeled and cut into 2-inch/5-cm chunks
- 2 garlic cloves, finely chopped
- 2 tbsp chopped fresh rosemary
- 2 tbsp chopped fresh thyme
- 2 tsp chopped fresh sage
- 3 tbsp olive oil
- salt and pepper
- 2 tbsp chopped fresh mixed herbs, such as parsley, thyme, and mint, to garnish

Preheat the oven to 425°F/220°C.

Arrange all the vegetables in a single layer in a large roasting pan. Sprinkle over the garlic and the herbs. Pour over the oil and season well with salt and pepper.

Toss all the ingredients together until they are well mixed and coated with the oil (you can let them marinate at this stage to let the flavors be absorbed).

Roast the vegetables at the top of the preheated oven for 50–60 minutes, until they are cooked and nicely browned. Turn the vegetables over halfway through the cooking time.

Serve with a good handful of fresh herbs sprinkled on top and a final seasoning of salt and pepper to taste.

Asparagus with Sweet *Tomato Dressing*

SERVES 4

- 5 tbsp extra virgin olive oil, plus extra for brushing
- ½ cup pine nuts
- 12 oz/350 g tomatoes, peeled, seeded, and chopped
- 2 tbsp balsamic vinegar
- 1 lb 2 oz/500 g young asparagus spears, trimmed
- ¼ cup thinly shaved Parmesan cheese
- salt and pepper

Brush a broiler pan with oil and preheat. Dry-fry the pine nuts in a heavy skillet for 30–60 seconds, until golden. Tip into a bowl and set aside.

Combine the tomatoes, vinegar, and olive oil in a bowl, and season with salt and pepper. Set aside.

When the broiler pan is hot, add the asparagus spears and cook for 3–4 minutes, until tender. Carefully transfer to a serving dish. Spoon the dressing over them, sprinkle with the pine nuts and Parmesan shavings, and serve immediately.

Fava Beans with Feta

SERVES 4–6

1 lb 2 oz/500 g shelled fava beans
4 tbsp extra virgin olive oil
1 tbsp lemon juice
1 tbsp finely chopped fresh dill, plus extra to garnish
2 oz/55 g feta cheese, drained and diced
salt and pepper

Bring a saucepan of water to a boil. Add the fava beans and cook for about 2 minutes, until tender. Drain thoroughly and set aside.

When the beans are cool enough to handle, remove and discard the outer skins to reveal the bright green beans underneath. Put the peeled beans in a serving bowl.

Combine the olive oil and lemon juice, then season to taste with salt and pepper. Pour the dressing over the warm beans, add the dill, and stir gently. Adjust the seasoning, if necessary.

If serving hot, add the feta cheese, toss gently, and sprinkle with extra dill, then serve immediately. Alternatively, set aside the beans in their dressing to cool and then chill until required.

To serve cold, remove from the refrigerator 10 minutes before serving to bring to room temperature. Taste and adjust the seasoning, if necessary, then sprinkle with the feta and extra dill.

Caramelized Sweet *Potatoes*

SERVES 4

1 lb/450 g sweet potatoes
½ cup butter, plus extra for greasing
¼ cup brown sugar, maple syrup, or honey
2 tbsp orange juice or pineapple juice
½ cup pineapple pieces (optional)
pinch ground cinnamon, nutmeg, or pumpkin spice (optional)

Wash the sweet potatoes, but do not peel. Boil them in a large saucepan of salted water until just tender, for about 30–45 minutes, depending on their size. Remove from the heat and drain well. Cool slightly, then peel.

Preheat the oven to 400°F/200°C. Thickly slice the sweet potatoes and arrange in a single overlapping layer in a greased ovenproof dish. Cut the butter into small cubes and dot them over the top.

Sprinkle with the brown sugar and the fruit juice. Add the pineapple and spices, if using.

Bake for 30–40 minutes, basting occasionally, until golden brown.

Honey-Glazed Sautéed *Squash*

SERVES 4

3 tbsp butter
3 tbsp honey
scant 4 cups diced winter squash
1 tsp finely chopped fresh thyme
salt and pepper
fresh thyme sprigs, to garnish

Put the butter and honey in a nonstick skillet and heat gently until melted. Add the squash cubes, chopped thyme, and seasoning and mix well. Sauté over medium heat for 8–10 minutes, turning and tossing frequently, until the squash cubes are tender and glazed all over (the glaze will gradually thicken and coat them). Garnish with thyme sprigs and serve as an appetizer with fresh bread, or as an accompaniment with broiled chicken, red meat, or fish.

Two-Potato
Puree

SERVES 6

- 2 large orange sweet potatoes
- ½ tsp vegetable oil
- 4 potatoes
- 2 tbsp butter
- ½ cup heavy cream
- whole nutmeg, for grating
- salt and pepper

Preheat the oven to 375°F/190°C. Rub the sweet potatoes with the oil, then bake in the preheated oven for 20 to 25 minutes, until tender.

Meanwhile, peel the potatoes, then cook in a large saucepan of boiling water until tender. Drain well and put in a colander. Cover with a clean dish towel to absorb the steam and let stand until cooled. Mash the potatoes or pass through a potato ricer.

Scoop out the flesh from the sweet potatoes and mix well with the potato in a warmed bowl. Discard the sweet potato skins. Melt the butter with the cream in a small saucepan, then pour half over the potato mixture and beat well with a wooden spoon. Add the remaining cream mixture a little at a time until you achieve the consistency you like. Season with salt and pepper to taste, and add a grating of nutmeg. Beat again, then serve.